Missing

True Cases of
Mysterious
Disappearances

Andrew J. Clark

MAPLEWOOD
— PUBLISHING —

Contents

They Just Vanished

Sometimes things happen that seem completely unexplainable. Life is normal and routine one moment, and then forever changed the next.

Just take the case of the mother who let her son go to the movie theater by himself—not only to have him disappear, but to have a complete imposter return in his stead!

This bizarre event—which is just one of the many cases we will delve into later in this book—inspired the 2008 film *Changeling*. In folklore, fairies were said to snatch children from the cradle and replace them with duplicates called changelings. According to this myth, parents would tuck their kid in at night, then wake up in the morning to find a similar but strangely altered child. They knew that something was different, but they couldn't quite place what it was.

While not all of the disappeared described below returned, the legend of the changeling could serve as an analogy for every one of the strange, tragic, and mysterious cases presented in this book. The lives of everyone involved in these events were somehow altered in ways they never could have conceived. One moment their lives were completely normal, but in the next that sense of normalcy had vanished forever—along with their dearly departed loved ones.

Ylenia Carrisi Disappears

Who: Ylenia Carrisi
When: January, 1994
Where: New Orleans, Louisiana

Context

Ylenia Carrisi seemed to be destined for fame and fortune from birth.

Born in Rome on November 29, 1970, Ylenia was the daughter of Italian celebrities Albano Carrisi and Romina Power. Her parents weren't the only famous ones in the family, either. Her maternal grandparents were actor Tyrone Power, of Golden Age adventure film fame, and his wife Linda Christian, a Mexican-American actress known for her roles in *Holiday in Mexico* and *Tarzan and the Mermaids*. Linda also holds the distinction of being the first "Bond girl"; she appeared in the first filmed performance of a James Bond story, a 1954 televised adaptation of the novel *Casino Royale*.

With celebrity running so thick in her blood, most assumed it would be just a matter of time before Ylenia took her own place among the glitz and glamour of the stars. And for a short while, she did indeed seem to be on the express track to stardom herself. While she was still in her late teens, she took the Vanna White role of turning letters on the Italian version of the American game show *Wheel of Fortune*. But Ylenia soon left the high road behind, took a detour, and veered into the ditch instead.

Her trip to the bottom of the barrel began with the most noble of intentions. With dreams of becoming a writer, she enrolled at King's College in London, where she received excellent grades during her first year of studying literature.

Soon afterward, however, Ylenia decided that she needed more inspiration than her studies at King's College could provide. In order to find it, she came up with the concept of traveling overseas on extended backpacking trips so that she could study potential subjects for her work in person and develop characters and plotlines based on her experiences. Taking a leave of absence from King's College, Ylenia returned to Italy and sold her possessions to raise money for her trip.

She then set off for Latin America, arriving in Belize in 1993. But within just a few months she had grown weary of life in this Central American country and decided to try her luck in the United States instead—in the French Quarter of New Orleans, Louisiana. She was already familiar with the city since she had vacationed there with her parents the previous summer.

This time, Ylenia arrived shortly after Christmas. She would disappear shortly thereafter.

According to those who remembered making her acquaintance in New Orleans, Ylenia quickly became involved with several local musicians and street people. One of these was a down-and-out jazz musician named Alexander Masakela. This Jamaican veteran of the New Orleans music circuit was 20 years Ylenia's senior. Not a whole lot is known about Ylenia's relationship with Masakela, but Masakela himself would later claim that they were merely friends who were not romantically involved.

Even so, the two had agreed to share a hotel room together, and this is where Ylenia presumably spent the last few days before her disappearance. Then, for some unknown reason, she abruptly decided to leave. She was never heard from again. Masakela stayed on for another week, without reporting anything out of the ordinary. But when he finally did check out, he attempted to pay the bill with Ylenia's own traveler checks.

The Day of the Disappearance

The exact day of Ylenia's disappearance is uncertain, but it was probably sometime in early January 1994. Some reports suggest the date as January 6th. Her parents last spoke with her by telephone on New Year's Eve / New Year's Day. After failing to hear from her in the following weeks, they reported her missing on January 18th.

The story takes some murky twists and turns from here.

It would seem reasonable to suppose that Ylenia's parents had had no reason to fear for their daughter's safety and were completely blindsided by her disappearance. But in the aftermath, some stories in the Italian news media made the sensational claim that, shortly before New Year's, Ylenia had visited her parents in Florida (where they were staying on vacation) and had mentioned a run-in with two nefarious individuals who had attempted to drug her. However, the tale is presented in such an unbelievable manner that it seems to defy common sense, and people familiar with Ylenia's parents have stated that they would never have allowed her to return to New Orleans if she had expressed any such concern.

Moving from speculation to fact, hotel staff stated that Ylenia checked out on January 6th without taking any of her personal property with her. She left her backpack, passport, and even all of her notebooks behind. The notebooks are of particular importance because they were where Ylenia had painstakingly recorded all of her observations of street life in New Orleans. Since this was her major reason for being in the city in the first place, it seems strikingly bizarre that she would part with them.

Just as strange, Ylenia's former roommate, Masakela, remained at the hotel until January 14th, and upon leaving he attempted to pay his bill with the traveler's checks that she had left behind.

The hotel night manager, Patty Eagle, confirmed these facts and also testified that she found the young girl and the much older man rather odd. While the pair were constant companions, Eagle did not feel that they were romantically involved. She remembered in particular how Ylenia had insisted that the two be booked in a room with two beds. Eagle's testimony thus supports Masakela's later assertion that he was not in a relationship with Ylenia.

At first, Ylenia's abrupt checkout and apparent disregard for her belongings was the only lead investigators had to go on. But on January 30th, a startling story from a security guard named Albert Cordova came to light.

Cordova was part of the security team at the Audubon Aquarium of the Americas, an aquarium-based theme park on the banks of the Mississippi River. He reported to police that while making his rounds at 11:30 PM on January 6, he encountered a young lady matching Ylenia's description sitting at the end of one of the park's piers.

Since it was after hours, she was trespassing, so Cordova confronted her and informed her that she would have to leave. She replied vaguely, "It doesn't matter. I belong in the water." The meaning of this odd proclamation immediately became clear when she then jumped off the pier into the Mississippi River!

Cordova stared in astonishment as the woman swam as hard as she could against the river's notoriously strong current. In a herculean feat, she almost made it to the other side, but then her strength gave out and she began to sink beneath the waves.

Realizing that she couldn't make it, she began to call out for help.

Cordova scrambled to call the police, but even as he dialed 911, he watched in alarm as a river barge sped by and sent crushing waves crashing down upon the struggling woman. He saw her go under—and simply never saw her resurface. The police showed up just minutes later and searched the entire area, even having a helicopter run a spotlight up and down the river, but there was no sign of the mystery woman.

According to Cordova's description, the woman he saw that night was a direct match for Ylenia. She was of the same age, same height, same weight, and had the same blonde hair and green eyes that Ylenia had. And besides these physical characteristics, the clothing the woman was wearing perfectly matched clothing Ylenia was known to wear. She was wearing a floral dress, cut just under the knees, and the same kind of jacket that Ylenia owned.

As you can imagine, this story has sparked all kinds of rumors and speculation. Those who believe the woman really was Ylenia have come up with several theories as to what it might mean.

The most obvious assumption is that Ylenia committed suicide. Some believe that she was depressed and perhaps overcome with guilt and shame regarding some of the rocky relationships she had been involved in—possibly including one with Masakela. However, the idea that she wanted to kill herself goes against Cordova's testimony that she cried out for help when she realized she could not reach the far bank of the river.

If Cordova's account is accurate, the woman's behavior was indisputably erratic. This has prompted many armchair psychologists to speculate that she must have been either mentally ill or under the influence of drugs. Why else, they ask, would a woman jump into the Mississippi River for no apparent reason?

One of the most intriguing theories, however, is that her mad dash across the river was simply to escape from Cordova himself. But if this is the case, to escape from what? It is true that she was trespassing on private property, but even if Cordova was going to have her arrested for it—which he wasn't—that hardly seems like a reason to risk life and limb swimming across the Mississippi! Proponents of this theory therefore suggest that the woman must have been up to something a little more than trespassing that night. Was she carrying some sort of illegal contraband on her person?

Of course, that's just wild speculation, and since it is rather impolite to speculate about unproven criminal activities of a woman most now presume to be dead, we will just leave that one for the armchair detectives.

Whatever the reason for this mysterious woman's decision to jump into those cold river waters that night, most people, including Ylenia's own father, believe that she was indeed Ylenia Carrisi—and that Albert Cordova was the very last person to see her alive.

The Investigation

From the day Ylenia was reported missing, the prime suspect was street musician Alexander Masakela. Known on the streets simply as Pops, this grey-bearded local jazz legend was already a person of interest in other crimes in the area. In fact, he was first questioned about Ylenia's disappearance in late January after being picked up for other offenses.

However, Masakela has always steadfastly denied knowing what happened to Ylenia. He contends he doesn't know anything more than anyone else: that Ylenia simply vanished without a trace.

It is true that Masakela has been implicated in violence against women on at least one occasion. Shortly after the police released him in January of 1994, Masakela found his way back into their hands when an ex-girlfriend renewed old charges of sexual assault. The charges were too flimsy to stick, however, and were soon dismissed outright.

The police, meanwhile, continued to search for new leads in the disappearance of Ylenia Carrisi, but despite their best efforts, no further clues turned up as to her possible whereabouts, and the case soon turned ice cold.

Update

Years later, in 2015, authorities made the surprise announcement to Ylenia's family of a possible new lead. The announcement came with a special request for Ylenia's father, Albano: They wanted to take a DNA sample from him. This was not because he was a suspect, but because his DNA would closely resemble Ylenia's own. This would make it much easier to determine whether human remains they were investigating belonged to her.

The new inquiry had begun when a Louisiana truck driver admitted to killing a woman in 1994. The woman had called herself Suzy, which was the name that Ylenia was going by shortly before her disappearance. The truck driver was named

Keith Hunter Jesperson, more infamously known as the Happy Face Killer. Jesperson confessed to Suzy's murder while he was being held on other charges. He claimed that he had picked the girl up at a gas station and murdered her shortly thereafter.

A body discovered in 1996 seems to back up this claim. The victim remains unidentified, but reconstruction of this Jane Doe's face from bone fragments is said to have created a stunning likeness of Ylenia. These new developments are still unfolding as of 2018, but hopefully soon a final determination can be made.

James Tetford's Bus Ride through the Bennington Triangle

Who: James Tetford
When: December, 1949
Where: Bennington, Vermont

Context

The story of James Tetford's mysterious disappearance actually begins with the previous disappearance of other members of his family. The story gets a little bit murky, but the gist is that James shipped off for duty in World War II and when he returned his wife and children were gone. You could just chalk this up to an unfaithful wife who abandoned her husband while he was overseas in the war, but the trouble is, neither she nor their children ever resurfaced. They apparently vanished without a trace.

Whatever happened to his family, the strain of their disappearance proved to be too much for James's battle-scarred nerves. In the years after his return to the U.S. he found himself increasingly unstable, bouncing from one halfway house to another. His final known residence was a veteran's facility called the Bennington Soldiers' Home. Although this was an assisted living center of sorts, James was apparently allowed some freedom of movement and even occasionally made trips to see relatives on the outside.

It was on one of these outings that James's own vanishing act took place. After visiting a relative in St. Albans, Vermont, he was taking a bus back to Bennington along with 14 other vets when he went missing.

13

Now, it's possible that James had grown tired of life at Bennington was simply seizing his last chance to escape. But even if the prospect of going back made him want to take off, the trip itself didn't provide much of an opportunity. According to the 14 other passengers, there was simply no time for James to disembark unseen. Instead, the man seemed to literally disappear right before their eyes. Everyone on board swore that James had been comfortably asleep, with all of his belongings nestled around him—and then suddenly he just wasn't there.

The Day of the Disappearance

World War II veteran James Tetford vanished without a trace on December 1, 1949. The date is significant since it marked the third anniversary of the mysterious disappearance of his family. Despite the ominous anniversary, however, he seemed to be in a good mood and had fallen comfortably asleep, apparently ready to take a nap for the rest of the ride. All of his belongings were in the overhead rack or on the seat next to him.

Only a few minutes after James had gone to sleep, alarmed fellow passengers looked over to find him nowhere to be seen. The man who had been slumbering peacefully moments before was gone. His suitcases were neatly stacked in the luggage rack, and his cash-filled wallet and his bus schedule were laid out on the seat next to his, but those were all that remained. No one saw him get up and leave, but when they happened to look over at where he'd been, James Tetford was nowhere in sight!

The bus had been moving at full speed down the highway the whole time, so even if James could somehow have gotten out without being noticed, it would most likely have meant jumping to his death. And even if he found a way around that peril (by climbing onto a getaway car?), it completely defies logic that he would have left his wallet. If he wanted to get away from

14

Bennington and start over somewhere else, you would think he would at least take his money along with him. The whole thing just didn't make any sense.

Of course, those who've raised the paranormal banner over this incident claim that where James went, money would be the last thing on his mind.

You see, the disappearance of James Tetford is just one of many that have occurred in the region. In fact, the disappearances have been so prolific over the years that they have prompted paranormal researcher and author Joseph A. Citro to dub the southwest corner of Vermont the "Bennington Triangle" in reference to the wide range of strange and mysterious events that have allegedly taken place in the area.

The focal point of this paranormal triangle is said to be Glastenbury Mountain. Many before James and after James have vanished on and around this local landmark, and coincidentally enough, it was right as the bus was approaching the nearest point on the route to Glastenbury Mountain that James himself disappeared.

Did he fall asleep, perhaps dreaming of his long-departed family, and then wake up in some other reality for a reunion? Did his sad life become just a bad dream that he was able to brush away as he wiped the sleep from his eyes? Or did James simply find a way to sneak off of the bus in a manner no one has been able to determine?

James Tetford is the only one who would know for sure, and he hasn't been heard from in about 70 years. We will most likely never know what happened during the course of this mysterious disappearance, but it continues to intrigue all who hear of it.

The Investigation

Immediately after the bus driver alerted authorities to James's disappearance, a massive search was executed in case he had somehow jumped or fallen out of the bus, improbable as that may seem. It proved futile, however, and no sign of James has ever been found.

Update

The case of James Tetford remained cold and forgotten for many decades. In the early 1990s, paranormal researcher, writer, and local folklorist Joseph Citro sparked new interest in this and other peculiar occurrences in what he called the Bennington Triangle by writing extensively about the incidents in his various paranormal anthologies.

Since then, public interest has mainly centered on the mysterious Glastenbury Mountain, where modern urban legend and ancient Native American folklore have congealed to produce a formidable mythology. But despite this renewed interest, when it comes to the disappearance of James Tetford, there are still far too many questions—and just about no answers whatsoever.

Harold Holt Goes for a Swim

Who: Harold Holt
When: December, 1967
Where: Melbourne, Australia

Context

Many of the tales of mysterious disappearances floating around the internet are so shrouded in mystery that it's difficult to be sure they happened in the first place. But if you would like to hear about a vanishing act that no one can deny, look no further than the former Prime Minister of Australia Harold Holt. When Prime Minister Holt vanished without a trace, you'd better believe that every printing press, television station, and radio broadcast in the world took note of the event. The simple but perplexing headline AUSTRALIA'S PRIME MINISTER HAROLD HOLT IS MISSING! raced across the globe after he failed to report to work on December 17, 1967.

PM Holt had assumed the office two years prior, and in that relatively short time he had managed to enact several liberal reforms for Australia. Most notably, he had shepherded the conversion of the outmoded monetary system based upon the British pound to one compatible with the U.S. dollar. Prime Minister Holt also shared U.S. President Lyndon Johnson's progressive views on racial equality and had carried out major reforms to put Native Australians on a more equal footing. In many respects, PM Holt was at the height of his career when he mysteriously disappeared.

The Day of the Disappearance

It was a clear day, without a cloud in sight, and to the Prime Minister of Australia, it looked like the perfect day to take a swim. Prime Minister Harold Holt arrived at Cheviot Beach on December 17, 1967, with a couple of his good friends and a couple of bodyguards in tow, ready to catch some waves. PM Holt himself was an avid outdoorsman who enjoyed snorkeling and spearfishing and was said to be a great swimmer.

The placid waves that the group encountered on that blissful day presented no challenge at all to PM Holt. And the shoreline at which they had set down their beach towels was one that he knew quite well. In fact, one of the last things he said that day was, "I know this beach like the back of my hand."

But despite PM Holt's mastery of watersports in general and Cheviot Beach in particular, there was a killer lurking beneath the deceptively placid surface of those waters. Cheviot Beach is known to have a formidable riptide current running through it from time to time. For this reason, coupled with the fact that PM Holt was still recovering from a shoulder injury, his bodyguards had warned him against swimming out too far.

But in typical, determined Harold Holt fashion, the Prime Minister brushed off their concerns. His friends recall him jovially ducking behind a large rock outcropping and emerging in his favorite pair of dark-blue swimming trunks. He then launched himself into the waters like a missile, displaying the swimming acumen for which he was famous. His shoulder wasn't bothering him, and as his confidence grew, he soon began to separate himself from his group and float further and further away from the shoreline.

Eventually his entourage lost sight of him. His companions climbed to the top of some of the rock formations jutting out of the beach to see if they could locate the drifting Prime Minister, but they had no such luck. After several more minutes passed without any sign of the PM, they alerted the Coast Guard. The Australian Navy and Air Force joined the search shortly thereafter, but it was all to no avail. This dashing and daring Prime Minister was never seen ever again.

The Investigation

After it became clear that Prime Minister Harold Holt was not going to be returning to the shore on his own, a massive search was launched to find him—dead or alive. First on the scene were local scuba divers, who tried their best to catch up with the missing Prime Minister. But the waves he had disappeared into proved to be too much for these men, and they were forced to return to the beach.

Soon afterward the police and the Australian Navy arrived on the scene and commenced the official search. Deep sea divers attached to Navy vessels by safety tethers forged through the choppy currents, and the Australian Air Force sent helicopters to scour the coastline, searching every inch of beach for the vanished Prime Minister. This amphibious mission became the biggest search and rescue operation in Australia's history.

The search was so exhaustive, in fact, and covered such a wide area, that after only two days' time, officials were able to declare with certainty that the Prime Minister was dead. According to the experts, if PM Holt was to be found alive, he would have been found already. And since Australia needed a new Prime Minister, it was decided that the death declaration had to be made sooner than later. John McEwen was accordingly sworn in to the now-vacant office.

But if Harold Holt really was dead, then where was his body? How is it that the search and rescue team could state with certainty that he was dead, but not have a corpse to show for it? Did they know something that the rest of the world didn't? These unanswered questions, of course, have generated an endless number of conspiracy theories from the very beginning.

Not helping matters was the fact that Australian law at the time forbade any official inquest into a disappearance unless a dead body was found. This created a bizarre catch-22 in which the Prime Minister was conveniently declared dead for the sake of continuity in Parliament, yet without a corpse, no one could look into his supposed death. This allowed officials to quietly sweep the whole matter under the rug—well, as quietly as possible for such a high-profile disappearance.

It wasn't long before whispers and rumors emerged blaming the Australian government itself. Some point to Holt's support of U.S. President Lyndon Banes Johnson and Australia's increasing involvement in the Vietnam War. During one of Holt's most famous public speeches, given in Washington, D.C., he declared a full commitment to the U.S., stating that he was "All the way with LBJ!" Many speculate that statements such as this led opponents of the Vietnam War to have him killed.

Another conspiracy theory implicating the Australian government relates to the mystery of the largest military base in Australia, Pine Gap. Pine Gap is sometimes referred to as Australia's Area 51, and paranormal investigators have long linked this base with UFO activity and strange and mysterious experiments of all kinds. Interestingly, just like Area 51, Pine Gap is said to be mainly run by the CIA, and some claim that the CIA ordered PM Holt's execution after receiving word of his desire to withdraw Australian support of the facility. The hit was then covered up as a tragic drowning.

Perhaps the most outlandish story to surface is that PM Holt was picked up by a Chinese submarine that had been patrolling the waters off Cheviot Beach. This strange story apparently originated with Australian Navy Commander Ronald Titcombe. Commander Titcombe relayed this story to the British novelist Anthony Grey, who then turned the tale into a fictional narrative entitled *The Prime Minister was a Spy*. Supposedly based upon what really happened to PM Holt, this book lays out an incredible story of subterfuge in which the Prime Minister of Australia himself is a double agent for the Chinese!

However, none of the investigations into Holt's disappearance in all of the subsequent decades have found any link to these preposterous tales—nor any further clues as to what actually happened to him.

Update

In 2005, due to changes in Australian law, an official inquiry into PM Holt's disappearance was finally made on behalf of his survivors. The conclusions of this inquiry were rather predictable: The PM had simply drowned, and his body, caught up in the rapid currents, was lost at sea. There was no mention of assassination plots by the CIA, or of Chinese submarines whisking PM Holt out of the ocean at the last minute. The facts, laid bare for the second time, only revealed a man who most likely misjudged the power of the ocean and lost his life at sea.

The specially designated Victorian coroner finally made it official, stating that Harold Holt was simply the victim of an accidental drowning and nothing more. December of 2017 marked the milestone 50th anniversary of this tragic event, and the sense of loss among Australians old enough to remember the incident is still palpable. Much like America's loss of President John F. Kennedy, the loss and mysterious disappearance of Prime Minister Harold Holt still stings—and still generates conspiracy theories to this very day.

Connie Converse Becomes Invisible

Who: Connie Converse
When: July, 1974
Where: Ann Arbor, Michigan

Context

The long-missing woman known as Connie Converse began life as Elizabeth Eaton Converse. The name Connie—like many things in this gifted artist's life—was just something that she picked up along the way. She was born on August 3, 1924, to a strict and austere Baptist minister and his wife. Despite the rigid rules of her upbringing, her family by all accounts was a loving one, and one that generally encouraged her endeavors in learning and the arts.

It soon became clear that Connie was a gifted student. She was the valedictorian at her high school graduation and won 8 out the school's 12 achievement awards for that year. Connie was the very definition of an overachiever, and her stellar achievements sent her on to college with a full-ride academic scholarship. In her freshman year Connie proved just as productive as ever, making top marks in all of her classes.

And so it seemed virtually unexplainable when she suddenly pulled out of her classes and quit college completely. Unbeknownst to her family and friends, Connie had taught herself to play guitar and begun writing songs. For most people, this might have been a mere escape from the rigors of academia, but Connie was different. This woman was truly gifted, and a quick learner, and it seemed that she soon became an expert at anything she set her mind to. She was already a skilled painter, sculptor and poet, so for Connie, suddenly turning her sights on the world of music was a serious pursuit—not just a phase or fancy.

Nevertheless, Connie's parents were understandably heartbroken to receive word that she had left college, and the decision created a rift that would last for the rest of her days. Connie was determined, however, and continued to plot her new course in life with a laser focus.

Setting her sights upon a career as a famous singer-songwriter, she packed up her guitar and went straight to the first place that aspiring singer-songwriters usually went in the late 1950s: Greenwich Village, in New York City. The Village at this time was giving rise to the Beatnik generation of artists who would become famous for their black turtleneck sweaters and poetically hip sentimentality. This cradle of creativity and the avant-garde was where Connie hoped she would thrive.

Unfortunately for her, however, it just wasn't meant to be. Connie's music, though appreciated by a small collective of friends in the Village, never did break out. This was a few years before Bob Dylan and folk music as a whole came to the forefront, and Connie's simple acoustic ballads just weren't gaining any traction. Her few fans gave her their full support, even getting her a gig on legendary news anchor Walter Cronkite's *CBS Morning Show* (which is now available on YouTube). Unfortunately, even this guest appearance on live TV failed to bring any follow-ups, and Connie continued what would be a long, slow slide into obscurity.

By 1961, Connie had all but given up on her dreams in music. Like some proto-star that had failed to ignite, she instead caved inward, collapsing under the weight of her own gravity. In silent resignation, Connie gathered her things and left New York for good.

At the behest of her brother Phil she headed to Ann Arbor, Michigan, where she rented out a modest hole-in-the-wall apartment. Phil was a professor at the University of Michigan and had promised his despondent sister that he would get her a job there and help her start a new life. With his help, Connie landed a job with the university periodical *Journal of Conflict Resolution*, and with the help of her shrewd intellect, she quickly worked her way up to editor.

Phil would later reminisce that Connie threw herself headlong into her work for the *Journal* but had sworn off music completely. After switching gears with her new role at the university, she packed up her once-treasured guitar and literally never touched it again. According to Phil, "After New York, she'd arrived at a place where she decided she wasn't going to make it, and in many ways that really hurt her." Sadly, Connie Converse internalized this heavy hurt, and while she tried her best to conceal it, the burden eventually became too much for her to carry any longer.

After a decade at the Journal, her coworkers began to notice that she was increasingly despondent and depressed. They were so concerned that they actually pooled their money for plane tickets to send her on an overseas vacation to London, England. This vacation somehow turned into an 8-month stay, but while there are some reports that she enjoyed her time in England, her mood did not seem to have improved in the slightest upon her return. If anything, she seemed even more depressed.

By now, even her estranged mother (her father had already passed on) was growing increasingly concerned about her daughter's mental state. Hoping to alleviate the crushing sadness that Connie felt, she invited her to go with her on yet another vacation, to Alaska. Connie told those close to her that she loathed the idea of such late-in-life mother/daughter excursions but felt she couldn't refuse. It would be an understatement to say that she went reluctantly. Phil, who escorted her to the cab that would take her to the airport, still remembers how his sister, before slamming the cab door, left him with the parting words, "I want to go to Alaska like I want to go to the basement!"

As one could imagine, the trip was not a very pleasant one for Connie, and shortly after her return things became even less pleasant for her. At a routine doctor visit, Connie was given the news that she would need a hysterectomy. She was in her late 40s at this point, unmarried and with no boyfriend, and had long since given up the idea of having children, but it still felt like yet another disappointment, like she was even more of a failure. As Phil recalled, "Connie still loved children, so I think she took that news pretty hard."

As the months wore on, she began to go about her affairs in a state of complete autopilot, just going through the motions. Yet unbeknownst to anyone around her, her placidly dour expression was hiding a fire within. As her 50th birthday approached in the summer of 1974, she had her own disappearance already planned out—and the only clue was an odd offhand remark to one of her nephews. This kid was a big Tolkien fan, and so in explaining her need to get away, Connie drew an analogy to *The Hobbit* and told him that just like Bilbo Baggins, she simply "had to go".

The Day of the Disappearance

Connie Converse's last words to her friends and family came in the form of written correspondence. In these last few missives, Connie jotted down a series of disjointed thoughts. Some expressed personal aspirations and others contained commentaries on current events such as the impeachment of U.S. President Richard Nixon. But she also included some more ominous portents in these letters.

In one, she tried to explain her failure to connect with others on a personal level: "Human society fascinates me and awes me, and fills me with grief and joy; I just can't find my place to plug into it." Along with such trenchant analyses of her awkwardness with others, she also gave more explicit hints as to her future plans. In one letter, she related that that she was considering a trip out West to "take another shot at life".

Although the exact day is not certain, it was shortly after she rattled off these final letters that she loaded up her small Volkswagen Beetle with a few belongings and left Ann Arbor, driving out of the lives of her friends and family for good. She was never heard from again.

The Investigation

By the time family and friends received Connie's last letters which insinuated that she was going to take off, concerned loved ones had already alerted the authorities. But the trail was cold from the very beginning of the search, and nothing turned up in subsequent months. No one with her name and social security number had applied for a job, been admitted at a hospital, incarcerated in a jail, or anything else. It seemed that wherever she might be—if she was indeed still alive—she was determined to stay off the grid.

About ten years after her disappearance, Connie's family finally hired a private investigator. However, this proved to be a complete waste of money because the selected shamus displayed a complete lack of zeal. In an epically egregious example of expectation-leveling, the detective began his search by telling Phil, "Look, I might well find your sister, but you need to know that if I find her, that doesn't mean she's coming back. It doesn't even mean that she'll talk to you." Predictably, he never did come up with any leads, and Phil and the rest of the family couldn't help feeling that the hundreds of dollars they had paid this phony would have been better spent somewhere else.

Update

After the disappointing experience with the private investigator, Phil put his sister's disappearance on the back burner. Realizing that the detective had been right about one thing—that Connie might not want to talk to him even if she was found—Phil resigned himself to wait on the off-chance that his sister might one day contact him.

Then, in 2004, a former friend of Connie's, New York music promoter Gene Deitch, played some of her old recordings on public radio. A couple of aspiring recording artists, Dan Dzula and David Herman, happened to hear the broadcast and were intrigued. They got in touch with Deitch and asked if he could hook them up with more of Connie's old recordings, and he happily obliged.

Since then, her songs have been re-released and one of her singles even became a number-one hit on Spotify. Wherever Connie Converse may have ended up, she's finally attaining the stardom and acclaim she longed for all those years ago—and hopefully, she's smiling.

The Lost Civilization of Percy Fawcett

Who: Percy Fawcett
When: April, 1925
Where: Amazon Rainforest, South America

Context

Colonel Percy Fawcett was one of the greatest explorers the world had ever known. A Briton living within the waning but still expansive British Empire of the 1920s, Col. Fawcett was determined to find new discoveries in a world that had already been almost completely mapped out. He had become fascinated with the wild and untamed jungles of South America, in particular the unexplored reaches deep within the Amazon Rainforest. This jungle covers some 2,300,000 square miles of northern South America, encompassing a large chunk of Brazil, substantial parts of Columbia and Peru, and small sections of Ecuador, Venezuela, and Bolivia. Such a vast region of unexplored wilderness was the ultimate enticement for an explorer like Colonel Percy Fawcett.

Col. Fawcett, born in 1867, was a man prepped and primed for adventure. He served with honor as a military attaché in British Sri Lanka for several years before moving on to espionage and intelligence gathering in North Africa. As a young man he was a kind of Victorian-era James Bond, but he soon showed that he could turn off his adventurous side and take on a more studious role when the occasion demanded. Shortly after these far-flung postings he hunkered down and lent his considerable intellect to the fields of archeology, geography and cartography (mapmaking).

The last of these led him to realize just how much of the world remained unmapped—and just how much of the unmapped portion lay in the jungles of the Amazon. In 1906 he got a chance to see the area firsthand when he was placed on a Royal

Geographical Society survey team tasked with mapping the no-man's land region on the border between Brazil and Bolivia, located in the western edge of the Amazon Rainforest.

This was the first of a series of expeditions that Col. Fawcett led into the rainforest. His fellow explorers were always amazed at both his expertise in navigating through the wilderness and the natural charisma and respect he displayed toward the local inhabitants. In an age when most high-born Englishmen looked down their noses at indigenous peoples, Col. Fawcett treated them as equals, according them the utmost respect and dignity. These good manners proved to be of tremendous benefit for his survey teams, making it much easier to gain the friendship and assistance of local populations during their exploratory missions.

Relying on his skills in navigating both the rough terrain and the finer points of tribal diplomacy, Col. Fawcett made a total of seven trips up and down the Amazon from 1906 to 1924. During these expeditions he took fastidious notes chronicling all of his encounters with massive snakes, huge spiders, and lively locals.

The public was enthralled by his tales, and by the time of his next major expedition, in April of 1925, the expectation had become very great. And Col. Fawcett himself was in the forefront of fanning the flames of publicity by claiming to be on the verge of finding an ancient civilization he referred to as the "Lost City of Z". From reading old accounts penned by Spanish conquistadors from the 1500s, and from his own conversations with the indigenous population, Col. Fawcett believed that if he pushed just a little farther through the jungle he would uncover a massive, previously unknown civilization.

Discovering previously unknown civilizations in the Americas was not unheard of—consider the sprawling complexes of the Aztec, Incan, and Mayan civilizations—and so the idea of yet another ancient city hiding in the Amazon did not seem unbelievably farfetched. Col. Fawcett theorized that shortly after the early Spanish expeditions spotted Amazonian cities in the 1500s, European diseases had all but wiped out these "urban jungle" populations. The thick foliage of the rainforest canopy had then covered up the abandoned city centers, hiding them from sight through the centuries.

Col. Fawcett found the theory entirely convincing and was absolutely determined to prove its truth. However, few of his contemporaries shared his certainty, and he was unable to assemble a large expedition. In the end, his party comprised only his 22-year-old son Jack, a friend of Jack's named Raleigh Rimmel, and a couple Brazilian guides. Col. Fawcett was traveling light, but he was dead set on returning to England successful in his mission. Unfortunately for him, he wouldn't return at all.

The Day of the Disappearance

Shortly before Col. Fawcett disappeared, he instructed his Brazilian helpers to return to camp. That left only himself, his son Jack, and his son's friend Raleigh Rimmel on the survey team. The three continued into the heart of the jungle—and never came out.

Percy Fawcett was 58 years old that day, and those who knew him had worried that his aging body would not be able to stand up to the rigors of the Amazonian environment. Still, he had been accompanied by two much younger men who would presumably have brought word if he had succumbed to some illness or injury. And so, from the very first, conspiracy theories about what actually happened to Col. Fawcett were abundant.

The first and most obvious explanation for Col. Fawcett's failure to return from the Amazon was that he had been killed or taken captive. Despite his adept maneuvering with native tribes, there were still plenty of indigenous groups in the region that were implacably hostile to all foreigners.

Others proffered the more fanciful theory that Col. Fawcett, who had always been enamored with the native lifestyle, had chosen to turn his back on Western civilization and join one of the tribes.

Even more improbable was the idea that Col. Fawcett had found exactly what he was looking for—the Lost City of Z—and either did not want or was not allowed to leave.

The Investigation

Col. Fawcett had left specific instructions not to send search and rescue teams after his party, but it wasn't long before follow-up expeditions were launched into the Amazon to find them. In fact, the hunt has lasted to this very day, and over 100 explorers have died in subsequent searches for Percy Fawcett and company. This is a staggering number, especially considering that Col. Fawcett pleaded with the public not to look for him should he not return. It almost makes one wonder if the reason why it has been so difficult to find any trace of Col. Fawcett is because he simply did not want to be found, and there are some who claim that he had every intention of disappearing into the jungle from the very beginning of his trip.

Some point to the personal notes he left behind, which detail not only his fascination with tribal life but also with the concept of shaping new tribal religions. Col. Fawcett was a proponent of Theosophy, a religious philosophy holding that there are many different paths to enlightenment. The name, which stems from Greek, means "Divine Wisdom", and Theosophy's adherents believed that there was a kernel of truth and divine wisdom to be found in every world religion.

Theosophy held that there were "ascended masters" in every religion who could aid in achieving enlightenment. Some believe that Col. Fawcett was seeking such ascended masters among the Amazonian tribes. Others go a step farther and suggest that Col. Fawcett made himself the high priest of a new religion he established among the native peoples of the rainforest.

Whatever the case may be, after a long and exhaustive investigation, no trace of Col. Fawcett was ever found, and no tribal group has ever claimed responsibility for his disappearance.

Update

In 1996, Brazilian adventurer James Lynch attempted to retrace the steps of Col. Fawcett's expedition. Along the way, he was captured by a hostile native tribe deep in the Amazon, and his group barely escaped with their lives. They only gained their freedom after convincing the tribal leader to accept nearly all of their possessions as "gifts" in exchange for their freedom and safe passage. After this run-in with death, the group radioed for help and was picked up by a helicopter and taken to safety.

This well-documented encounter certainly lends credence to that idea that Col. Fawcett met his fate at the hands of hostile inhabitants of the Amazon, but there is still no real proof as to what befell the great explorer.

The Disappearance and the Changeling of Walter Collins

Who: Walter Collins
When: March, 1928
Where: Los Angeles, California

Context

Much has been written about the strange missing persons case of Walter Collins, and there was even a 2008 movie loosely based upon his disappearance. Walter was just a boy when he vanished, and he was a boy very much loved by his mother, Christine Collins. From the day he disappeared, she was beside herself with grief and desperate to get her son back.

Even before she lost her son, Christine had had a far from charmed life in early-20th-century California. The daughter of a poor Irish immigrant, she had worked several menial jobs before marrying a conman and petty crook who went by the name of Walter Collins but whose real name was actually Walter Anson. It was from this union that young Walter Collins was born. In 1923, Walter's father was arrested for his many con-jobs and sent to Folsom State Prison. He passed away behind bars shortly thereafter, leaving Christine to raise Walter by herself. It was under these already trying circumstances that Walter Collins went missing on March 10, 1928.

The Day of the Disappearance

Little Walter Collins disappeared on the 10th of March, 1928, after his mother gave him some money to take in a couple of films at a nearby movie theater. He walked out of Christine's door to watch a movie—and simply never walked back in. She called the LAPD almost immediately and a manhunt ensued, but the police were unable to find any sign of Walter Collins.

The Investigation

After a five-month investigation, police were not any closer to finding out what had happened to Walter Collins than when they had begun. After months of searching, all they could say was that Walter might have run away. Christine found this explanation both unhelpful and offensive, because she knew that her son would never willingly have left home. She knew that if her son was missing, it was because he was being held against his will.

Christine was not the only one unhappy with the LAPD at this point. The department was already suffering from a long spate of bad publicity for corruption and bungled cases, and their inability to find anything substantial in the Walter Collins investigation was leading to mounting public pressure. The man in charge, Captain J.J. Jones, was therefore eager to latch onto any lead he could find. In this atmosphere of grasping-at-straws desperation, the police were primed to seize upon the first possible break in the case that came up—no matter how improbable.

At first all they had to go on was a couple of witnesses who'd seen a boy matching Walter's description getting into a large automobile of some sort in the company of an "Italian" man and woman. Further investigation revealed that the same "Italian" man had been asking around Walter's neighborhood for the boy just a few days before. But this seemingly promising lead fizzled when neither Walter nor the Italian couple alleged to have been holding him could be found, and the investigation came to a dead end until August.

Then, out of the blue, the police finally received the break they'd been looking for. A boy claiming to be Walter had been found in DeKalb, Illinois, alive and well.

39

As you can imagine, Christine was overjoyed and immensely relieved. She shelled out her own hard-earned money to put the boy she believed to be her long-lost son on the first train home. The story generated massive media coverage which drew huge crowds to the train station, where an excited audience awaited the touching reunion of mother and son.

Unfortunately for Christine, however, things did not turn out as anyone expected. The second the boy stepped off that train, she exclaimed out loud to everyone in earshot, "That's not my son!"

Now, a mother would normally be credited with the ability to identify her own child, but the fanfare about Walter's return and the expectations of the crowd that the boy would *be* Walter were so great that many among them seemed inclined to force this false narrative upon poor grieving Christine.

The police, too, were so eager to close the case that they were ready to accept Walter's return as reality whether his own mother was willing to or not. Captain Jones himself stepped into the mix and insisted that Christine look at the boy again. When she still protested that the child was not hers, Captain Jones informed her that she was mistaken. He suggested that the child probably just seemed different after several months of growth and the trauma of his disappearance.

An increasingly upset Christine adamantly informed the LAPD officer that she would know her own son if she saw him. Captain Jones, however, refusing to admit that his department had made a mistake, insisted that Christine at least take Walter home and, "try him out for while". In this bizarre case, the LAPD seemed to be treating a child like a puppy that Christine just needed to try out for a few days before deciding whether to take it back to the pet store! Even more astonishingly, under this immense pressure, Christine, although certain that the boy was not her son, felt forced to take him home to "try out" anyway.

But as much as the police had mismanaged the case so far, they were at least professional enough to follow up with "Walter" about what had happened to him and how he had wound up in Illinois. In a series of interrogations by police investigators and child psychologists, the boy raised more questions than he answered. He could not describe his abductors, explain how he had escaped from them, or even account for his out-of-state trip. The boy seemed to draw a big blank as to what had occurred during the past few months.

The investigators could only conclude that either he had amnesia, or he was being purposefully deceptive. Not wishing to upset their superiors, they settled for the amnesia theory until they could find more information.

In the meantime, Christine took the boy into her home and tried her best to get acquainted with him, but deep down she never believed that he was her Walter. She soon found a means to prove it by getting a copy of her son's dental records and comparing them with the new boy's teeth. It was obvious that they were indeed two separate sets of teeth; they simply did not match.

Christine took her findings to Captain Jones, but it only seemed to infuriate the officer. Throwing the evidence down on his desk, he accused her of attempting to make a mockery of the LAPD. After seizing the dental records, he then had Christine declared a safety risk and involuntarily committed to a psychiatric hospital. Unbelievably, just because this woman refused to believe the lie being foisted upon her, she was being declared insane by the LAPD! At this facility she was forcibly restrained and plied with all manner of psychotropic drugs. Even though she was perfectly sane when she went into the ward, the hospital staff seemed determined to drive her crazy before she got out!

Such an egregious abuse of power in a twisted conspiracy between police and hospital administrators seems truly incredible. As much as the LAPD has been criticized for corruption in more recent times, it would appear that the LA cops of the 1920s had sunk to a level of depravity that would have shocked even Rodney King. It is absolutely horrific what this poor woman was put through just because she couldn't accept the false findings of her friendly neighborhood police department.

Thankfully, she survived this onslaught long enough for her freedom to come. It came in the form of a confession. Ten days into her confinement at the psych ward, the boy who had been pretending to be her son finally broke down and admitted that he was not Walter. His real name was Arthur Hutchins Jr., and he was actually a runaway who had latched on to the Walter Collins story to get a free ticket out of his own troubled home life.

After this stunning admission, the authorities had no choice but to release Christine, send Arthur back to his real parents, and reopen the investigation into Walter's disappearance. By now, though, the trail had grown even colder. Buried under layer upon layer of bungling, investigators didn't even know where to start. They were at a complete standstill until rumors of the worst kind of crimes began emanating from a ranch in Wineville, California.

Authorities had received reports that the ranch owner, Sarah Louis, and her adult son Gordon Northcott were abusing children held captive on their property. Police raided the ranch, but the deranged pair had fled the premises. They did find some abused children, however, and one of them, a boy named Sanford Clark, informed them that he had seen Walter Collins among their number—and that he had been killed by Louis and Northcott. The police searched the ranch and dug up some human bone fragments but could find no complete skeleton. The reason, they were informed, was that Northcott had dismembered his victims' bodies in the desert.

More telling discoveries included library books with missing children's names on them, along with their clothing, which was found inside the chicken coop. Louis and Northcott were captured soon thereafter, and both confessed to their crimes, admitting to the slaughter of at least 20 children in what would become known as the Chicken Coop Murders (since their victims were held captive inside the chicken coop). Northcott got the gas chamber for his role, while his mother was sentenced to life in prison. But even though it was presumed that Walter Collins was one of the victims of the Chicken Coop Murders, neither his body nor parts thereof were ever found.

Christine, wishing to find out the truth for herself, arranged a meeting with Northcott shortly before his execution and demanded to know if he had indeed killed her son. Whether he couldn't bring himself to confess to the boy's own mother or whether it was the sincere truth, Northcott replied that out of all the children he had murdered, Walter Collins was most certainly not among them. Christine chose to believe the final words of this mass murderer, and to her dying day she considered her son to still be missing, still holding out hope that one day he would be found.

Update

There have not been any real breaks in this case in recent years, but in 2008 interest in the story was reignited by the film Changeling, which was loosely based on the Walter Collins case. This epic movie directed by Clint Eastwood sheds light on the fraught emotional dynamics of the real-life drama that intertwined a corrupt policeman, a distraught mother, and a serial killer back in 1920s California.

Finding Fard

Who: Wallace Fard Muhammad
When: December, 1934
Where: Detroit, Michigan

Context

The man who went by the name Wallace Fard Muhammad is
perhaps the most mysterious figure of the 20th century—so
mysterious that no one knows his real name, where he came
from, or where he went after he disappeared without a trace.

Fard seemed to have appeared from nowhere when he began walking the streets of Detroit in 1930. He presented himself as a door-to-door salesman of silk garments. Most of the poor, inner-city homes he visited could not afford to buy his wares, but Fard was selling more than silk—he was also selling ideas. The silk he held in his hand was usually just a way to get his foot in the door, and after presenting the garments as having been made by the best silk weavers in Africa, he explained to his eager listeners that there was a whole world they knew nothing about, in which people like them lived like kings and queens completely free of the racial oppression and discrimination that was rampant in 1930s America.

This was of course music to the ears of those who were so sadly downtrodden. Fard soon became quite popular in Detroit, and he was regularly invited into people's homes to teach his exotic beliefs. He soon developed an entire unique ideology that put the racism of the day completely on its head. He explained to his audience that they had been deceived, that it was the African people who were the true masters of the Earth, and that Europeans were an inferior subspecies created by a mad African scientist name Yakub 6,000 years ago.

This claim sounds absolutely laughable to today, but back in the 1930s, when eugenics was all the rage, Fard found a fascinated audience. His listeners were more than ready to accept his ideology that Europeans were a bad strain of stock escaped from an ancient African laboratory, and that these "white devils"—as Fard sometimes simplified the description—were the source of all their woes. As his movement—otherwise known as the Nation of Islam—began to gain traction in Chicago as well as Detroit, police attention increased apace, and soon Fard was even on the radar of the FBI.

Things came to a head when one of his temple[s] out elaborate rituals that may or may not have inc[lude] sacrifice or two. In any event, his teachings were view[ed as] being highly subversive. Local police began to apply pres[sure] and wherever Fard went, he was quickly told by the authorit[ies to] leave. Realizing that he was no longer in a position to head the movement he had founded, Fard appointed a successor named Elijah Robert Poole, otherwise known as Elijah Muhammad, and moved increasingly into the background. Eventually, he left town for good. Elijah Muhammad saw him board a plane at the Detroit airport—and that was the last anybody saw of him ever again.

The Day of the Disappearance

The exact date is unknown, but Fard allegedly executed his vanishing act sometime in 1934 by getting on a flight out of Detroit. Only his young protégé Elijah Muhammad accompanied him to the airport, and according to him he begged Fard to stay "with tears in his eyes". Fard, however, insisted that he had to go. He gave Elijah Muhammad a list of books to read, ordered him to carry on the teaching of the Nation of Islam in his absence, boarded a plane, and left.

The official stance of the Nation of Islam, which holds Fard to have been much more than an ordinary man, is that he left this world entirely. The movement's current leader, Louis Farrakhan, who has repeatedly expressed his interest in UFOs, has also expressed his belief that Fard is most likely aboard an alien spaceship touring the cosmos.

The mythos behind Fard has become rather far-fetched, but the more believable explanation for his disappearance—the one gleaned from leaked FBI memos—is hardly mundane either. The FBI's version states that Fard had been linked to a murder carried out by one of his followers, and had been given an

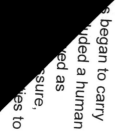

e the city or face charges. Whether he
simply fleeing from criminal charges, his
arrival, remains a complete mystery.

ɔn

ɹaintain Fard's file, but there wasn't much to
ɹance in 1934. In 1958, however, due to
increased ɑɔʈɪ⋯ɪ., ɹ Nation of Islam under Elijah Mohamed, the
FBI delved into Fard's past once again and made what they felt was
a significant discovery. They found striking similarities between the
Fard persona and records of a California man named Wallie D.
Ford.

Ford had been arrested twice, once in 1918 for assault with a
deadly weapon and again in 1926 for violation of the California
Poison Act. His conviction for the latter came with a sentence of
one to six years in prison. FBI agents surmised that when Ford
suddenly appeared in Detroit as Fard, it was probably immediately
after his release from prison, meaning that he must have served
four years, from 1926 to 1930, before launching his street ministry.

Furthermore, the FBI compared two sets of fingerprints, one from a
1933 booking of Fard and one from an earlier arrest of Wallie D.
Ford. According to the FBI, these two sets of prints for two men with
slightly different names were an exact match. The FBI officially
closed its investigation into Fard less than a year later, on April 15,
1958, and no further inquiry into Fard's whereabouts has been
made since.

Update

Leaving aside rampant speculation, there have been no further
developments in this case, and Fard's disappearance remains a
mystery to this very day.

The Missing Physicist

Who: Ettore Majorana
When: March, 1938
Where: Naples, Italy

Context

Ettore Majorana was one of the foremost physicists of his day.
Born on the Italian island of Sicily, Ettore began his life in the
simple, slow-moving world of the Sicilian countryside. His brain,
though, turned out to be anything but simple and slow-moving.
While still in his teens he was recruited to join a group of whiz
kids called the Via Panisperna Boys. The group's leader was
perhaps the most famous Italian physicist of them all—Enrico
Fermi.

When he began college, Ettore was already on the fast track to becoming a top-notch physicist. Still working closely with Enrico Fermi, he helped to discover the slow-moving neutrons that would soon make nuclear reactors possible. Ettore was in fact on the cusp of making a grand finding in this area, but after he unwisely failed to take Fermi's advice to publish his ideas, another young physicist by the name of James Chadwick beat him to the punch and took the Nobel Prize for his work.

Ettore's inspiration and insight apparently deserted him after this setback, and he settled into a routine life as a professor of physics at Naples University. With no major breakthroughs forthcoming, his life seemed destined to be one of relatively accomplished obscurity in academia. This would all change, however, when Ettore decided to make a seemingly spontaneous trip to Palermo, Sicily, from which he wouldn't return.

The Day of the Disappearance

For reasons that are still unknown, Ettore emptied his bank account days before his scheduled trip. Of course, if Ettore was seeking to run away from his circumstances and start a new life for himself, taking his money with him would make complete sense. But wherever he ended up, there is no evidence that he ever spent it.

Another, more ominous, sign that Ettore wasn't planning to return was the letter he left for the University of Naples Director of Physics, Antonio Carrelli. It read: "Dear Carrelli, I made a decision that has become unavoidable. There isn't a bit of selfishness in it, but I realize what trouble my sudden disappearance will cause you and the students. For this as well, I beg your forgiveness, but especially for betraying the trust, the sincere friendship and the sympathy you gave me over the past months. I ask you to remember me to all those I learned to know and appreciate in your institute, especially Sciuti: I will keep a fond memory of them all at least until 11 PM tonight, possibly later too."

The reference at the end to keeping a fond memory of his colleagues "until 11 PM" is rather odd, to say the least. It could be interpreted as a reference to suicide, an indication that Ettore planned to end his life by 11 PM. But seeming to contradict this interpretation, Ettore sent out a telegram later that night suggesting that he was getting ready to return to Naples. Not only that, he had already purchased a ticket. But there is no record that he ever made this trip, and this was the last communication he ever made. Ettore took to the seas on Friday, March 25, 1938, and was never seen again.

The Investigation

In the immediate aftermath of Ettore's disappearance, investigators were completely baffled. They had no idea as to why this brilliant physicist would suddenly disappear. A massive search was conducted throughout Italy, but no leads were found, and the investigation was soon abandoned as the shadow of war began to loom over Europe.

Update

An incredible update to this case came in 2008 when a caller to an Italian TV show featuring Ettore's strange disappearance offered a tantalizing new lead. This caller, an Italian named Francesco Fasani, claimed that he had actually met Ettore in South America back in the 1950s. Fasani said he had been working as a mechanic in Venezuela when he made the acquaintance of a man who went by the name of "Mr. Bini" but was actually none other than Ettore, who had been hiding out in nearby Argentina. What's more, Fasani claimed to have proof and brought forth a 1955 photograph showing a man strikingly similar to Ettore Majorana.

Intrigued by the new findings, the office of Rome's Attorney General announced that it would reopen the case. And in an announcement that stunned the world, after analyzing the photo and all other relevant data, on June 7, 2011, it was declared that "ten points of similarity" could be found between the 1955 photo and previous known photographs of Ettore.

Then, on February 4, 2015, it was officially announced that there could be no doubt that Ettore and the man depicted in the photograph from 1955 were one and the same. As far as the Italian government is concerned, this missing persons case had been solved—although there are still many who would disagree.

The Band Leader Goes Missing

Who: Glen Miller
When: December, 1944
Where: English Channel

Context

Glen Miller was a band leader who rose to fame in the 1930s with masterful big band pieces such as "Chattanooga Choo Choo" and "In the Mood". He was a patriot as well as a musician, and after the United States was dragged into World War II, he committed himself to do all he could to boost the morale of the troops. From 1942 until his disappearance in December of 1944, he traveled to dangerous hotspots all over the globe to give American GIs a small reprieve from the fighting.

By the end of 1944 the Allies had all but defeated the Axis powers. Italy had already been knocked out of the war, Germany was on its last legs, and Japan was boxed into a corner. The Americans, British and Russians were on the verge of victory, and when Glen was scheduled to perform in liberated France, it promised to be the safest venue on his itinerary in years. With American might controlling the land, sea and sky, no one expected any trouble.

And if the prevailing theory is true, it wasn't enemy action that took down Glen's plane—it was the exceedingly bad weather.

The Day of the Disappearance

On Christmas morning, 1944, Glen Miller boarded a single-engine plane with a crew of two. He was flying to join the other members of his band who were waiting for him across the English Channel. They were scheduled to give a surprise concert for the troops. It was a kind of last-minute Christmas gift from the top brass, and Glen didn't want to disappoint his fans. But shortly after takeoff, all communication with the plane ceased, and the three men who were on board were never heard from again.

This mysterious disappearance of one of America's greatest performers in his prime has generated never-ending speculation and conjecture.

Of course, the most obvious reason for the plane's plummet into the English Channel would be the area's endemic bad weather. Glen had actually been advised to cancel the concert for just this reason, but not wishing to disappoint, he had insisted that trip go ahead as planned. Visibility was horrible, however, with fog as far as the eye could see, so flying conditions were certainly not at their best.

Another plausible theory is that Glen was knocked out of the sky by friendly fire. This is one case in which it is actually quite reasonable to postulate a conspiracy, because the military obviously would not wish to let it be known that they had accidentally blown the most famous American musical icon of his day out of the skies!

And there are, of course, some even more outlandish theories floating around. One has Glen being captured by the Nazis, and according to another Glen secretly *joined* the Nazis. However, there is absolutely no evidence for any of these wild theories outside of someone's fevered imagination.

The Investigation

The first investigators into Glen Miller's disappearance concluded that his plane had accidentally gone down due to the fog and poor visibility over the English Channel. This theory would be vigorously debated in the 1980s, however, when reports came to light that a Royal Air Force flight had been returning from an abortive bombing run over Germany at the exact same time that Glen's plane was flying over the Channel. This led to speculation that the British planes had accidentally bombed Glen's smaller, lower-flying aircraft while releasing their unexpended munitions into the sea.

Update

In 2017, it was discovered that a man from Devon, England, had documented Glen's flight in a diary he had kept as a small boy during World War II. The diary contains an entry which indicates that the youth spotted Glen's aircraft. Notably, the time and coordinates that the young man jotted down do not match those previously ascribed to Glen's flight path. This evidence makes it more likely that Glen's disappearance was due to either mechanical trouble or pilot error.

Susan Walsh and the New York City Vampires

Who: Susan Walsh
When: July, 1996
Where: Nutley, New Jersey

Context

Susan Walsh's number-one aspiration in life was to be a writer, but her path towards this goal was a bit unconventional to say the least. She paid her way through college by working at various strip clubs, and she picked up a nearly devastating addiction to drugs and alcohol along the way. Fortunately, she was eventually able to overcome these problems, get clean, and receive her degree.

Susan married Mark Walsh in 1988 and gave birth to their son David shortly thereafter. Soon after the birth of her first child, with several years of sobriety under her belt, she began to pursue her passion for writing once again by penning articles for scientific trade journals.

As Susan's professional career began to pick up, however, her personal life became more tumultuous. She separated from her husband a few years later. It's not clear if Susan's penchant for stripping was a factor in the divorce, but shortly afterward Susan Walsh went back to her old life as an exotic dancer to help bring in extra money for her and her son.

She continued to write, however, and even landed an internship with the famed New York paper *The Village Voice*. When the editor proposed a story on connections between the Russian

Mafia and New York's sex industry, Susan's personal experience in the field made her the perfect person to tackle it. And she did not disappoint. Using her extensive connections, she was able to infiltrate deep into the seedy world of New York City's Russian-run strip clubs, and her article won her great acclaim. She had finally gotten the recognition she had long craved.

But she had also made some powerful Russian mobsters very upset with her coverage of their activities. Soon after the article's publication, Susan became convinced that she was being followed. She also told close friends that she had received a few unspecified threats.

Nevertheless, Susan plowed ahead to her next journalistic endeavor, beginning work on an article about New York City's underground vampire scene. This was a subculture of young people who enjoyed gathering together and pretending to be vampires. She once again had a personal connection to the subject matter, since she was currently dating a man who believed that he was a vampire! But apparently for this very reason, the *Voice*, citing a lack of objectivity, ultimately declined to publish the article.

Needing to make up for the lost income, Susan went back to stripping. Ironically, she also appeared in a documentary called *Stripped*, produced by a friend of hers named Jill Morley, which decried the sex industry and the objectification of women. After Susan's disappearance, Morley testified that Susan had become increasingly unstable. She cited Susan's diagnosis of bipolar disorder and her history of mental illness, as well as the fact that she had recently stopped taking her medication.

This testimony was supported by John Ridgeway, a *Village Voice* editor who had also noticed Susan exhibiting erratic behavior. He related that Susan once came to work with her wrists heavily bandaged as if she had recently attempted suicide. Ridgeway also said that Susan had fallen off the wagon, abandoning her years of sobriety and delving into heavy drinking once again. When he asked her about it, she basically told him it was none of his business and that she would ask for help only if she needed it.

Along with all of this personal instability, there was the instability of her relationships. Susan had chaotic relationships with men for most of her life, and at the time of her disappearance she was in an undoubtedly strained romantic situation: She was sharing an apartment with her 21-year-old boyfriend Christian Peppo while her ex-husband lived directly below. She also had an obsessed ex-lover who was habitually stalking her, so much so that she had to file a restraining order against him. This ex-lover is also alleged to have assaulted Peppo on at least one occasion. It was in this swirl of personal and interpersonal chaos that Susan Walsh vanished.

The Day of the Disappearance

At noon on the 16th of July, 1996, Susan told her boyfriend Christian Peppo she was leaving to make a phone call. Cell phones weren't yet common, and Susan apparently didn't have a home phone, so she frequently used payphones. She instructed her boyfriend to put on a movie for her son and told them that she would be right back. There was a payphone just a block away from the apartment, but instead of heading there, Susan—demonstrating just how complicated her life was—stopped off to visit her ex-husband downstairs.

She had decided to ask him if she could use his phone to save herself the walk. But when she mentioned that the call she wanted to place was to the agent who handled her exotic dancing gigs, Mark steadfastly refused. One can hardly blame the man for refusing to encourage the mother of his child to strip, but sadly enough, if he had simply allowed her to place that call from the safety of his apartment rather than from a payphone on the street corner, Susan might still be with us today.

Because after she stormed off, slamming the door in her ex-husband's face with a testy "Fine!", she rushed off to that payphone and walked out of her loved ones' lives for good. In her haste to place the call, Susan had left all of her personal items behind. She had no wallet and no form of identification. And when several hours passed and she failed to return, it was clear that something was terribly wrong.

The Investigation

Susan's ex-husband Mark first reported her missing on July 17, 1996, when she failed to return home from her trip to the payphone. The first thing the police did upon hearing that she had walked to a payphone was naturally to trace the phone calls made from that phone. Strangely, they found that Susan had never placed any calls that day.

After this angle fell flat, the next step in the investigation was to look into the ex-boyfriend with the restraining order. But as far as the police could tell, the ex-lover and sometime stalker, for all his faults, had not been anywhere near Susan's apartment on the day she disappeared.

Next on the investigators' agenda, as is usual in missing persons cases, were those who interacted closely with Susan on a daily basis—her boyfriend Christian Peppo and her ex-husband Mark Walsh. But both men were cleared early on in the investigation.

With the three most likely men all eliminated as potential suspects, the mystery of what had happened to Susan Walsh deepened. Police were made aware of Susan's substance abuse problems, which raised concerns that she might have overdosed somewhere. Her editor at the paper, John Ridgeway, considered this the mostly probable explanation for her disappearance, saying, "I think she probably went out and called somebody to come and get her and then she went, and she may very well have overdosed." But searching through the streets and alleys near Susan's home did not turn up any body, dead, comatose or otherwise.

Strangely, the police detective in charge of the case soon developed the strong opinion that Susan had simply wandered away on her own. As he said at the time, "For some unknown reason, she opted to leave her family and home, which she has a perfect right to do." With this belief already cemented in the minds of the chief investigator, police were not exactly overzealous in seeking new leads in the case.

Update

The next development came a month after Susan disappeared. Her friend Mellissa came forward to say that she had seen Susan standing on a street corner next to a black limousine. Susan actually looked up and saw Mellissa, but when she called out her name, Susan quickly got into the limousine and the car took off at full speed.

This intriguing sighting became a concrete lead because Mellissa had had the presence of mind to jot down the limousine's license plate number. The police were thus able to contact the driver. When shown a picture of Susan, the man confirmed that he had in fact seen a woman who looked like her, but he was unable to provide any more useful information.

Several more possible sightings of Susan followed over the next few years. Many of them were reported by prostitutes who suggested that Susan had fallen victim to human trafficking. The theory then began to develop that Susan had been ensnared into prostitution by the very Russian Mafia that she had angered with her article.

Was Susan really picked up by the Russian mob and forced into prostitution as retribution? It's been over two decades since her disappearance, and there have been no further updates. Whatever may have happened to Susan Walsh, no one seems to be talking.

The Strange Case of Jamie Fraley

Who: Jamie Fraley
When: April, 2008
Where: Gastonia, North Carolina

Context

Jamie Fraley, a native of North Carolina, was last seen in the vicinity of her residence at the Copperfield Apartments in Gastonia, NC, on April 8, 2008. Jamie was a young woman with a few challenges. She was diagnosed as being bipolar and suffered from frequent bouts of anxiety. Although she was 22 years old, she had never managed to obtain a driver's license, and as a result she depended on friends, neighbors, and even her social worker for rides. When she came down with a bad case of stomach flu on April 8th, she was forced once again to rely on the kindness of others in order to get herself to the hospital.

The Day of the Disappearance

On the day that Jamie disappeared she had become sick with severe stomach pain. Unable to drive herself to the emergency room, she called a friend to take her to the hospital, then called her mother to tell her what was going on. She did not, however, identify the friend by name, and whoever this mysterious "friend" was, it appears that they never took Jamie Fraley to the hospital as promised. Jamie herself seemed to have every intention of coming back right back, since she had left her keys, wallet, purse, and ID card at her apartment.

Even more disturbingly, two days after her disappearance, her cellphone was found on the side of the road a few miles from her apartment. It seemed as if someone had simply thrown it out of a car window as they drove by. Police immediately seized the phone as evidence and noted that many calls had been logged on the day of Jamie's disappearance, April 8th, as well as early in the morning of April 9th. After finding this phone, authorities were almost certain that some kind of foul play was at work, and they began an intensive investigation into Jamie Fraley's disappearance.

The Investigation

Initially the police were hopeful that fingerprints could be gleaned from Jamie's discarded cellphone. Unfortunately, by the time investigators got the phone, too many other people had already handled it. There was no way to differentiate one smudged fingerprint from the next. The calls logged on the phone did not prove to be of much relevance either.

With the recovered phone leading them down a dead end, investigators turned their attention to Jamie's close associates. Jamie had a boyfriend named Ricky Dale Simonds Jr., but he was completely safe from scrutiny since he had been incarcerated at the time of her disappearance. Her boyfriend's father, on the other hand—Ricky Dale Simonds Sr.—became a person of interest almost immediately.

Ricky Dale Sr. was an ex-con with a long rap sheet, and he just so happened to live and work at Jamie's apartment complex, where he was responsible for building maintenance. Besides his close proximity to Jamie, the fact that Ricky Dale Sr. had prior convictions for violence against women, including charges of strangling an ex-girlfriend, made him a prime suspect. Ricky Dale Sr. had also been known to give Jamie rides from time to time, so it seemed entirely possible that he was the "friend" who gave her that last, ill-fated ride she had told her mother she was waiting for.

Police immediately questioned Ricky Dale Sr. and asked him to submit to a lie detector test, which he refused to do. They continued to investigate him as a person of interest, however, seeking any evidence that might implicate him in Jamie's disappearance. But this investigation led to a quite literal dead end when Ricky Dale Sr. was found dead in the trunk of his ex-girlfriend's car.

Now, normally when a dead body is found in a trunk, investigators zero in on the car's owner as the most likely perpetrator. But in this case, knowing Ricky Dale Sr.'s history and the fact that this ex-girlfriend had a restraining order against him, police settled on an alternative narrative of events. They concocted the theory that Ricky Dale Sr. hid himself in his ex-girlfriend's trunk with the intention of ambushing her the next time she opened it.

If this were the case (and many justifiably believe that it was not), Ricky Dale Sr. must have been expecting his ex-girlfriend to open the trunk quickly enough that he could avoid being cooked to death in its sweltering hot interior—but this was not the case. It's not certain how long Ricky Dale Sr. was inside that trunk banging and screaming to be let out before he succumbed to the intense heat, but after his ex-girlfriend reported the discovery of his body, her story was accepted with no further investigation and no questions asked.

To be sure, neither the police, nor the ex-girlfriend, nor even Ricky Dale Sr.'s own estranged son—Jamie's boyfriend—were all that sorry to see him go. Nonetheless, investigators felt that his death dealt a devastating blow to the Jamie Fraley case.

They believed that Ricky Dale Sr. had been the only person who could potentially help them find answers about Jamie's disappearance.

Update

In 2015, Jerry Douglas Case, a man already in prison for murder, claimed that he had killed Jamie Fraley back in 2008. His jailhouse confession stated that he had killed both Jamie and another woman that same year. However, records indicate that Case was locked up in prison when Jamie went missing, making his involvement impossible.

So why would Case confess to a crime that he did not commit? According to District Attorney Locke Bell—just to "play games". DA Bell elaborates that people facing life sentences throw out fake confessions all the time in order to get media attention or use their "information" as a bartering chip to negotiate better conditions in prison.

Accordingly, authorities refuse to entertain the idea that Jerry Douglas Case could be the killer. It seems that they had identified Ricky Dale Sr. as their man, and even the gruesome discovery of his cooked corpse in the trunk of a car gave them no reason to change their minds.

Avraham Mengistu

Who: Avraham Mengistu
When: September, 2014
Where: Gaza/Israeli Border

Context

Avraham Mengistu was born to a Jewish family in the East African country of Ethiopia. Citing religious persecution, his parents sought and were accepted for asylum in Israel. Ironically, they shared a name with the Communist dictator from whom they fled—Mengistu Haile Mariam, who had overthrown the last Ethiopian Emperor, Haile Selassie, in 1974, violently ending one of the world's oldest dynasties.

The Mengistu regime ushered in a period of harsh collectivist rule, full of persecution and famine, which lasted until Mengistu's overthrow in late 1991. Although they shared a name, Avraham Mengistu's family benefited from Mengistu Haile Mariam's disastrous regime no more than anyone else. After pleading for asylum, they were brought to Israel in the Ethiopian exodus known as Operation Solomon.

The family was grateful for their second chance, but Avraham was slow to adjust and soon developed what his family describes as "mental challenges". These challenges increased after his older brother Michael, who served in the Israeli Defense Force, passed away in 2012. Avraham idolized his brother, and with his passing, all efforts to control his mental instability ceased. Avraham stopped taking his medication, and his behavior spiraled out of control. At one point, for example, for reasons known only to himself, he took a piece of string, tied it around his finger as tightly as he could, and left it there until blood flow was cut off and gangrene set in. The finger had to be amputated.

Due to such bizarre behavior, Avraham was admitted for evaluation at a psych ward in Beersheba, located in southern Israel, in January of 2013. He spent a little over a week in the Beersheba facility, and just five days after his release his family had him forcibly committed once again due to an increase in his odd and erratic behavior. During the following year Avraham continued to lose his grip on reality. He would ramble incoherently from topic to topic, on subjects that made very little sense. Then, in the fall of 2014, after what was to be his last nonsensical diatribe, he stormed out of his worried family's life for good.

The Day of the Disappearance

Avraham Mengistu disappeared on September 7, 2014, after asking his mother for cash—and becoming upset when she refused to give him any. Before anyone could stop him, he ran away from the family home and headed for the heavily guarded (and restricted) Israel/Gaza border. Israeli guards saw him crossing the border, but to the later surprise and consternation of Avraham's family, they didn't attempt to stop him right away.

The guards explained that they had assumed Avraham was a Sudanese refugee and figured that he had simply decided to return to Sudan through Gaza. But when a security camera showed that Avraham had just scaled a security fence, they decided that it was time to act. By the time that they arrived, however, Avraham was already hopping over the fence. They were too late.

They shouted for him to stop and turn back, and even fired warning shots over his head, but Avraham completely disregarded them and ran in the other direction. In his haste to scale the fence he had dropped the bag he was carrying, and the troops took note of its contents. He had only a few miscellaneous books, a pair of slippers, a towel, and a copy of the Holy Bible. This testimony of these two Israeli border guards was the last report of Avraham's whereabouts to reach the outside world on the day of his disappearance.

The Investigation

Immediately after Avraham Mengistu crossed over into Gaza, the Israeli government implemented its standard "10 months of silence", requesting that information about the incident not be broadcast by media while officials quietly tried to obtain Avraham's release. They soon learned that Avraham was being held by the terror group Hamas in the Gaza Strip, a fact confirmed by a Hamas leader shortly thereafter.

He informed them that Avraham had been detained and interrogated according to Gaza authorities' standard procedure for any Israeli crossing their border. The Hamas official went on to state that all the interrogation had revealed was that Avraham was a mentally unstable and deeply troubled young man. But no matter what his mental difficulties may have been, for Hamas he was still a suitable bargaining chip that had fallen into their lap. And soon enough, Hamas leadership began demanding the release of several of their members being held by Israel in exchange for Avraham Mengistu.

While these negotiations dragged on, the 10 months of enforced silence passed, and Avraham's family spoke out to the public for the first time. The first major organization they contacted was the International Red Cross, whom they asked to investigate what else could be done to secure their troubled relative's release. Via the Red Cross, they provided documentation of Avraham's troubled mental state, proof of his need for medication, and an official declaration that he was in no way, shape, or form part of the IDF or involved in any military operations.

It was hoped that once Hamas saw that Avraham posed no threat, he would be released. But unfortunately, despite the best efforts of both the Israeli government and international humanitarian organizations such as the Red Cross, Avraham does not appear to be any closer to coming home.

Update

So far, the only real update in this case is that the Israeli government decided to release security video that shows Avraham entering Gaza. This video proves that Avraham crossed the border voluntarily, but evidence that the mentally unstable man left Israel of his own free will does nothing to assuage the grief of his anguished family. As his mother put it, "I would have preferred to see footage of my son Avraham Mengistu returning home. My son struggles with mental health disabilities, and there is a daily concern for his life. The delivery of the recording does not exempt the state of its responsibility to return my son to his country."

Avraham Mengistu's family is still waiting for that day of his return.

Looking to be Found

It's a sad reality, but statistics show that thousands of people mysteriously disappear without a trace every single year. The reasons for this are many. Some may have met with foul play, others may have chosen to end their lives in secluded areas, and still others may simply have gotten lost. As this book has shown, there are many disappearances that just don't have any easy answers. Anguished family members have spent entire lifetimes searching for their missing loved ones to no avail. But as heartbreaking as such circumstances may be, in the end there is no one who is truly lost—just those who are looking to be found.

Further Readings

As we bring this book to a close, I wanted to take the time to share with you some of the reference and reading materials that were an integral part of my research. Here you will find a complete listing of the sources that helped bring this text to life. If you would like to learn more about any of the stories presented here, or even fact-check some of the statements made, please feel free to examine any or all of these great resources and references in full.

The Lost City of Z: A Tale of Deadly Obsession in the Amazon.
David Grann
This incredible book documents the path of modern-day researcher, author, and explorer David Grann as he attempts to retrace the steps of the British adventurer Percy Fawcett who disappeared into the Amazon a century before. In this book Grann compares and contrasts his own experience with what Col. Fawcett must have gone through. Along with this insight he provides a fairly strong historical summary of Col. Fawcett's life and adventures. The book also provides some tantalizing updates about the case, such as the 1996 expedition—the last real attempt to locate Col. Fawcett—and its near disastrous results. If you're looking for an in-depth telling of all things related to Percy Fawcett, this book is an excellent start.

Green Mountain Ghosts, Ghouls, and Unsolved Mysteries.
Joseph A. Citro
This book's author, Joseph A. Citro, is an expert on folklore from the Eastern Seaboard and the man who coined the term "The Bennington Triangle" in regard to the hotbed of paranormal activity allegedly present in the state of Vermont. In this book Citro relays odd stories of disappearances within this triangular region that seem to defy any rational explanation.

One of the seemingly paranormal vanishings that Citro describes in depth is that of James E. Tetford, the World War II vet who took a nap in the back of a bus and seemed to literally vanish into thin air right in front of his fellow passengers.

If you would like to explore missing persons cases that seem to go beyond normal human explanation, this book provides a plethora of detail and a wealth of knowledge about some of the stranger and even more mysterious disappearances that have allegedly transpired in the area.

The Life and Death of Harold Holt. Tom Frame
Here in this book Mr. Frame lays out the entire life of this ill-fated statesman. If you would like to learn more about any aspect of the Australian Prime Minister's life, from fact to conspiracy-theory fantasy, this book is a comprehensive resource on Harold Holt. Learn just how this brilliant man and resourceful politician, cut down too soon, impacted the world during his life and through his death.

The Vermont Monster Guide. Joseph A. Citro
This is another good book by Joseph A. Citro. Here he expands upon the more unusual subject matter of Vermont folklore and historical record in a rather campy and entertaining fashion. If you would like a good read about some of the more interesting myths and legends of the region, take a good look at this book!

Majorana: Unveiled Genius and Endless Mysteries. Salvatore Eposito
If you would like to read an in-depth biography on the life and subsequent disappearance of the brilliant physicist Ettore Majorana, this book takes you through all the important milestones. It has proven to be a crucial reference point, and much relevant data has been gleaned from this text.

Glen Miller Declassified. Dennis M. Sprag
A true expert in the field, Mr. Sprag takes us through all of the events leading up to the tragic disappearance of America's greatest band leader. This book is riveting in its portrayal of Glen Miller's last days. If you would like to better understand what may (or may not) have happened to Glen Miller and the crew that accompanied him over the English Channel, this book is a must read!

www.websleuths.com
This site is an invaluable resource for missing persons cases of all kinds. It provides up-to-date information on a case-by-case basis, and you can find direct timelines to events as they have occurred. This site has provided a wealth of information for just about every chapter in this book. If you have any questions, or would like to check on any of the details presented in this text, www.websleuths.com is a great resource to use.

www.mysteriousuniverse.org
Mysterious Universe, as the name just might imply, is a fantastic resource for everything—well—mysterious! And it won't let you down when it comes to missing persons cases, either. This site has compiled a wide variety of stories and anecdotes of mysterious disappearances and is worth at least a brief read-through.

Also by Andrew J. Clark

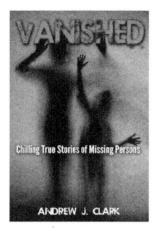

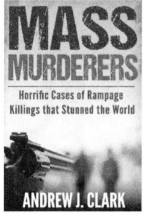

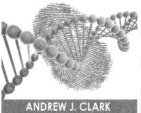

Printed in Great Britain
by Amazon

28163363R00046